INSIDE OUT

RENU SINGH PARMAR

DEDICATION

I dedicate these poems or soul verses, as I call them, to all those lovely souls
who inspired them.

Contents

Contents

Preface

I began writing poems as a 10-year-old and found them to be the best way to resolve my growing up pains.

Whatever needed a resolution or needed to be changed or seemed absurd or too difficult to understand would need to be penned down immediately. Needless to say some of the most emotive poems came straight from the soul as if somebody else and not I was writing. That's why the collection is called 'Inside Out'....that which comes spontaneously from inside, from the soul. It is, effectively, a collection of 'soul verse' by a young girl growing up into a thoughtful, somewhat cynical woman. The poems included in this anthology have been penned during the period 1974 to 1995.

Most of these poems appeared in my debut book of poems, *Ovarian Sentiments,* published way back in 1993. However, some have since been edited and others, which I found in some old notebooks and diaries, added.

Renu Singh Parmar

Acknowledgements

The illustrations in the book have been taken from the Pixabay website, majorly the works of artist
Bianca Van Dijk. The cover has been designed by a brilliant eleven year old boy, Rannvijay Singh Parmar !

Inside Out

SOUL VERSE

1. Indian Girl 1974

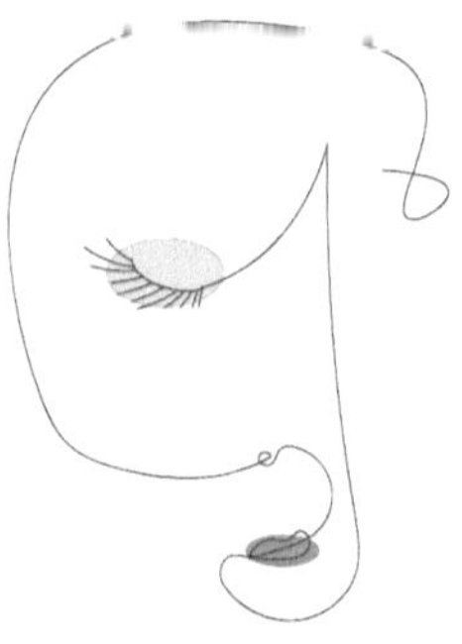

After all, what is communism to me,
I have no political inclinations.
Who said I was a Marxist, Leninist,
or any one of those?
I exist, I guess that's enough.
I'm just another Indian girl,
and I should know cooking.
I'm just a sweet teenager
treading gingerly on adult paths,
wanting to be conversant in newspaper pessimism,
and revolutions' blood baths.
But I am wasting my time,

the way you waste yours,
my dear friend, working out chemical reactions.
Besides, your future life is in a test tube,
all ready made, a bit of this , a bit of that,
calculated by parental fractions.
You'll forget your chemistry lab,
And I, my red commie flag.
After all, we are both Indian girls,
we shouldn't forget that.

2. Rain God

When the rains did not come,
and the land began to crack,
they started their murderous chanting,
a salutation to their God above,
an obeisance that would buy them rain.
They beat their dholaks to give
heartbeat to their pleading:
Oh God ! give us rain,
let this not be in vain,
give us rain,
even if it means
taking one of us.
The drums beat faster,
they created a ladder of shouts,
to lead them to God,
to get there first.
The madness peaked, prayers began howling,
cymbals clashed, heads started rolling.
Their God above looked on with a grimace,
and sent them rain in a tearing hurry.
This certainly was blackmail,
this, the price of His glory.

3. One- Way Street

Love was a one-way street
I so foolishly blundered upon,
that finally, when my remains were collected
after accidents of faith
of trust,
of hope,
of belief,
there was nothing much left,
so that if love had ever been,
it fled the skies of dawn,
it fled from verse, from smile.
Fled-fled away to some obscure corner of life,

the corner where I sit sometimes,
contemplating sadly
the demise of tenderness,
pondering over the could-have-been,
and laughing resignedly at love's losing labour,
telling myself that perhaps,
everything isn't fair in love and war
after all.

4. Routine Death

Again someone has gone
and left relatives weeping,
to fill up a vacuum somewhere,
with his youth rendered futile.
He went away without protest,
with some final gasps.
But here's eternity in certainty:
you can't win against sure odds,
unless you're winning a losing battle.

Dazed mother with glazed eyes,

cringing from reality:
He can't be dead, NO!
Sister's crying,
thank goodness for that,
and father looks on at the helpless heap,
his son: see my son, look at him sirs.
Mother says Sai Duba will retrieve him.
People cry,
ladies whisper sobs into the silent air
as men stand sentry over him.

We tug at our anchors
and trudge wearily home.

5. The Unsung Life

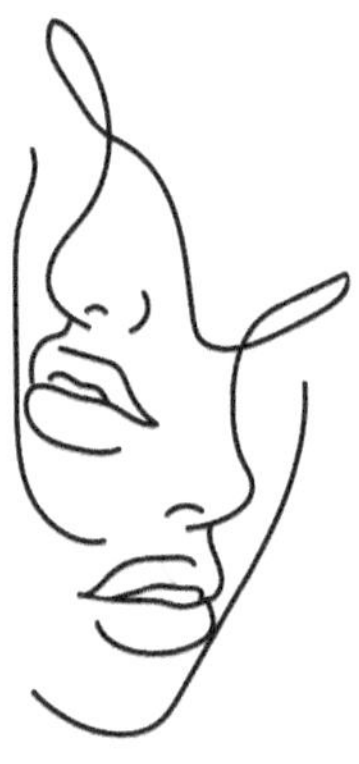

When I was born
my grandfather did not salute
the event with gunfire
as he thought he would
had I testosterone.
With my ovarian built
I was also granted the colour
of the night
I was born in-
starless, dark, mystical, dangerous.
His eyes did not sparkle,
his mouth did not smile,

when I let out my coming-to roar,
for him, I was just an eyesore.
Today, life proceeds, still
unheralded, untrumpted, unsung;
all the kegs of gunpowder
lying wasted, unused.

6. Ghazals

I

Having loved you so, I cannot love you more,
for my love is not like the unfaithful moon
that waxes and wanes with circumstance.

II

That I did love him for so long, he did not know...
You did not tell me, he says simply,
But how could I, how could I?
Love's not easy at confession,
My love, he lacks consideration!

III

My love says he knows what love is,

saying he knows not what it is, in the same breath!
How am I to believe what I would,
when my love knows not what he believes.

IV

Even as love made me, it unmade me too,
How cruel, how foolish are its ways!
But my love says love is not foolish;
What does he know about love,
if he knows not love's foolery?
Ah, but it is vain to imagine
that he knows love,
for my love flings the word without
caressing it on his lips.

V

How often he tells me not to worry:
everything will be alright, he reassures.
He knows not, then, what love means.
He knows not that love does not cure.
How shall I not worry,
when love has become a worry?
For I know he loves me not.

7. Wanting To Grow Up

As with the years, life grows complex,
so do the ways of the simpleton,
and what was thought to be maturity
reveals itself as a mirage-a desert quirk,
a desert quirk, no more.

For, maturity, like utopia
is limitless, undefinable, desirable.
It is but conjecture of wishful mind,
and of curious thought.
There is nothing, I say, like maturity,

what the hell are we groping at?

Each new step is the toddler's experience,
one learns, one unlearns, one begins to know
that which seemed so easy
is not one day's show.
That each step is a limp and no more,
that there are many, many miles to go.

Growing old back into childhood,
we start off again at square one,
for in learning we learn the infinite truth:
this is the beginning, just the start,
there's no more life to learn living's art.

8. Just a Fling

Tenderly he takes my hand,
A bit rattled at his guts,
Then, without warning, asks me:
Do you know why a boy holds a girl's hand?
Those hazel eyes melt in their own mirth
And scan my face for some revelation,
Which I hide with some consternation.
Then he weaves a web of inanities
And traps me in them,
And when I try to retrieve this hand of mine,
He holds on so, he won't let go!
I then shrug at his puzzle,

And see puzzles in those eyes.
His answer is not all that wise:
"It's a pleasure to hold your hand."
Well, at least you've shed your guise!

9. In Memory of Vivek Sharma

Here it is again: death,
and we wonder why it must be.
Who knew what lay ahead
when he woke up this Holi morning.*
As he came to meet his friends,
he met with death instead.
It's death we fear, not God.
Gods can be got in photo frames,
laced in smiles of benevolence.

These gods are dead;
we have lost our heads:
we ask for life and we meet with death.
And so, God, you left him in a heap,
After you'd used him after you abused him.
When sobs ring out in hospital corridors,
you look on helplessly,
grinning sheepishly from your photo frame.
It's such a shame, God, such a shame!
From now on you have no name.

*(*Holi is the Indian festival of colours)*

10. When She Married

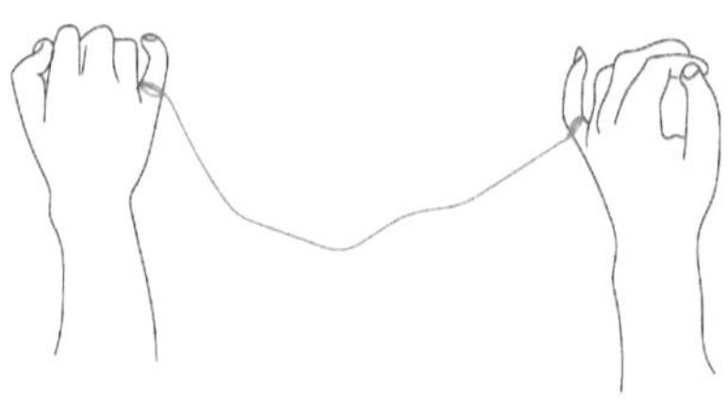

She has gone, breaking off these routine ties
for something more splendid.
Her needs now need never come begging
at my door;
After all, I was just a friend.
But now she has much more, much more —
it was not mine to lend.
Today something leaves her as it leaves me,
our well-worn friendship sheds its garb,
and here we are again
like strangers that have met before in a dream,
memories licking the vacant corners of our hearts.
Her familiar ways, like her bindi

newly ensconced on her forehead,
move away from me,
and are for somebody else now.
Our old ways will grow white
and crystallize into the past.
Friendship will now be
more of something from the past,
[illegible]

11. The Rules of the Game

Eventually, I've come to this conclusion:
these monotonous loves of mine are my eternal
quest for the real romance, ye olde romance.

Here crumbles the air castle of another
one-sided tamasha,
Here go all the hopes I had painted
onto a prostitute's lips.
Because even if your acceptance lingers somewhere,
I know I shall always have this feeling
of rejection,

this continuous worry of my
first love's defection.

The shadows of love are no longer soft,
menacing, they menace me:
Stay away, you fool,
this game is not for you,
you don't even know the rules.

12. A Woman Scorned

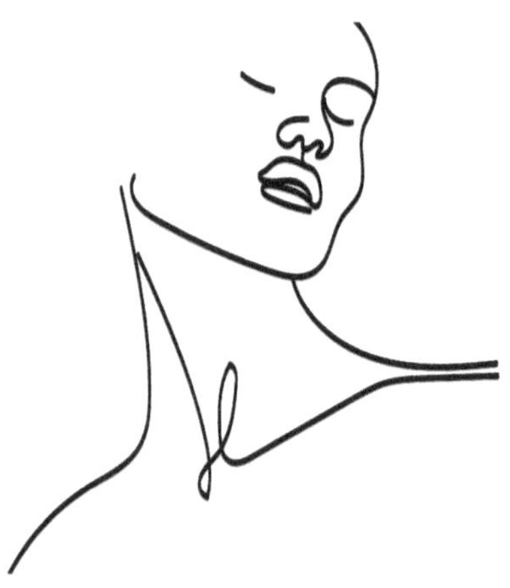

When all the embers of a virgin life
have died down,
and I have borne some kids for the making of a family,
there shall still be
in this mad mind of mind
a bitterness you sowed very early.

I shall seek you out for my revenge,
and you, having lost yourself
in a fruitless cohabitation,

will want something meaningful
and find it only in me.
Yes, yes, that just has to be!

And when I see those needs of yours
staring me in the face,
and when I see my image
mirrored in your desires,
you'll find you've fallen from grace,
you'll be burning in your fire!

13. Catharsis

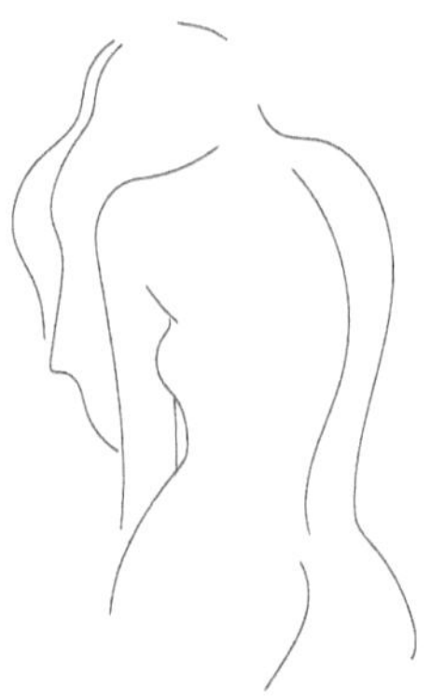

Beyond the corners of the mind
must lie reasons beyond all seasons,
No springs, no summers, no monsoons, no winters,
just the withered hues of worn-out passions,
things that go beyond all fashion.
Untimed, untimely, they creep up
towards hearts ventilation
and, with a few tears, are dealt with peremptorily.
Left to rust they defy all rules
and rise once more, when I am alone,
when I am more prone

to their stings and bites of maliciousness.
We all have a viciousness in us
That breaks all regulations,
that erupts at unwilling catharsis,
that unnerves all our meditations.

14. Shame

What promises could lie in the eye of another?
I give up this guessing game, this waste of time,
this ridiculous shame.
When the emotions in you
Reach out and touch me,
can't you complement them with words?
and must I search for meaningless platitudes
in your silence?
It's just not fair –
am I such poor ware
that you cannot even caress my needs
with your voice?

Do I really have no choice?
Must I always face silence,
must I always seek to borrow
the promises in my tomorrow
from others certified not mine?

15. Shameless

It wasn't many days back when I said:
I can flick off guys like ash from a cigarette.
But here I am holding onto thoughts of you.
And, yes, it's true,
That I can need even you
Who cannot speak out loud
For fear of saying too much.
For, we dislike creating scenes,
we dislike so much to disrupt
The orbits of our worlds,
to create scandals,
and be termed, vandals
in this arena of love
which we haven't even seen yet.

16. A Women's Love

I know that even as I sit here,
Crumpled in this lamp-lit corner
Thinking about your possible disassociation
with me,
you will be unthinking of the girl
you left behind.
But I am a woman now, and my desires
want more than merely your presence:
yes, I want to feel the touch of
your smile in me,
I want your breath to breathe
the fragrance of love in me,

I wish to know the corners of your heart,
the silent spaces of your emotions.
I want to feel the openness of your arms,
the greatness of this thing called union with you.
In a man, libido is an ember that bursts
suddenly into flames, dies out just as soon.
A woman's passion builds up with longing,
and glows like smouldering cinders,
always and always.

17. You and I

When you are gone even a few days,
I find I tire easily,
I get bored, I am easily irritated —
for somewhere in my mind
I can locate the gaps you leave behind.
Gaps of emotion which you fill-up
with the touch of your smile, your smell,
your very ownness.
Do you realise how much love you give me?
Maybe unwittingly — but even though
you don't say those words,

you say them every now and then
when, unconsciously, you admit
that you need me for everything.

18. Office Hours

I

Stagnation

Like a dying clockwork toy
the dull life proceeds limp by limp,
to finally stagger and perhaps fall.
Our dreariness has a base
in the monotones of lonely lives,
the monochromes of colourless dreams.
We sit around idle tables,
contemplating the murder of our souls,
cold tentacles of sweat

stagnating into brittle icicles.
The crumpled drafts of ambition
in the dustbin say it all:
There is no way out of here,
caged, confined in the flaps
of routine office files, we'll never get out of here.
For, here, there are only culs de sac to enter,
only broken ladders to climb.

II

Irrelevance

Our notions of self-respect come in package deals
of plush offices, swivel chairs, salam Mem Sahib.
A musty, claustrophobic office, with rickety furniture, bare floor,
with sad and drooping time for company
makes for no self-respect.
It makes only for disgust, discontent,
Envy, disenchantment.
Like misguided youngsters
we sit and discuss red carpets, and wood panelling,
while the major issues sigh and rot in our files.

III

Ennui

The incessant clatter of typewriters,
and of bored voices over the telephone,
the groan of dangerously unstable fans,
the drone of dying aspirations,
all swirl in this centrifugal ennui
that has come to stay.
Between endless cups of office tea

one ruminates the demise of enthusiasm
that goes with the beverage.
With relentless routine,
one gulps down insipid realities, mincing at the dryness
in throat, eye, mind, body.

19. It's a Girl

It's a girl, too bad!
Third in the line,
unlucky woman, she wasn't blessed
to have sons.
And this man, her husband,
Says so what,
Ladki hui to kya hua*
It's okay with me.
You women want sons,
providers in your old age.
You women want bahus,

to dispose of as you wish.
All of you have a patriarch,
a mother-in law in you somewhere.

**hindi for: so what if it's a girl?*

20. Starvation Deaths in Orissa

Somewhere in this land
mango kernels, boiled carcass
become a feast.
The last supper –
For after the betrayal, the eternal sleep.
Our desperations label us human,
As we try to ignore the hearsay:
it can't be – why exaggerate?
there are no reports of starvation deaths,
we can give relief doles, anyway,
the situation is under control.
The government monogram stamped in blood

appears on unrelenting sarkari faces.
Reporters vomit and wince:
Heck, what a shitty place!
How putrid can we Indians get?
Anyway, what a scoop!
And pens like this
swagger at the opportunity of morbid verse,
rendering death literary.

21. Till Next Time...

When we touch
mind to mind, body to body,
soul to soul
Peace floods my veins –
I stockpile your whispers, your touch,
the textures of your body,
your moods –
filing them carefully under wraps
in my subconscious –
to be drawn out,
laid before me,

for a languid re-past
which I may allow myself
in some remote tomorrow
when you are not here
or when I miss those quiet exchanges,
when breath mingles
into an expanding stillness,
a calm brought about by
the surrender of the mind, the soul.
When I lie next to you,
your quietness engulfing mine
Our eyes heavy with the drink of love,
I know that we have met
before in the pages of a story
that happened before….
We meet again,
as we must -
to fulfil the strong pull of our destinies.
And perhaps continue
even in the next chapter
yet to be written.

22. To a Friend

Your icy logic leaves me cold,
I can't understand the automation
that dictates tick-tock in your mind,
your words so precise, so exact —
like an executioner at work
You cut my throat with your precision.
Your structured world is difficult to understand,
it falls into well-fitting spaces,
contoured just right.
The numbras and penumbras of my mind
however, cannot see it in that light.
I've loved the openness of space

in my moods, mind, heart.
The confines of your exactness,
like a claustrophobic dream, scares me.

• 43 •

23. Rejection Slips

Our kitsch dreams scream for recognition,
Like prostitutes they wear red
and flaunt a lust they're not sure of.
They stop strangers on the road and solicit them:
Try me, have a go,
I won't let you down,
please don't say no.
But there are no takers, no buyers...
They push us away hat in hand,
A donkey clap as reprimand.

24. Anger

Do you realise how I burn with anger?
I burn and burn and consume myself,
eat into my brain, my sane mind,
destroy peace and create fear.
I can do all that – I do it in anger.
My demons are so predictable, raising their heads
without warning, without any contemplation,
– even I am taken aback,
– taken back, I regress:
childlike tantrums, uncontrollable fits,
Of bad language, crude expletives.

The pounding of tongs at my temples,
the raised voice, heartbeat,
the snarl of animal unable to think,
and my toddler cringing in a corner,
hands over his young head in self-defence,
my servant neurotic with attacks of
stomach trouble, breathing trouble,
ear trouble,
– I am the cause
I cause the anger.

25. Obsession

Not learning from past errors,
I go round and round in circles
unable to break away from my obsessive ways.
You too,
have your peculiar ways
of circling around like a vulture,
waiting for the kill.
Can someone put a stop to this?
It is making me too dizzy.
I can see only the blurs of
the all too familiar patterns

kaleidoscoping into the same shapes,
even as I try to extricate
myself from the grip
of this madness.
But no-
You won't let me
and I won't let you...
this see-saw will continue
till one of us collapses,
till the roller coaster slows down
out of sheer fatigue,
and the monstrosity
crashes into oblivion.

26. After the Madness

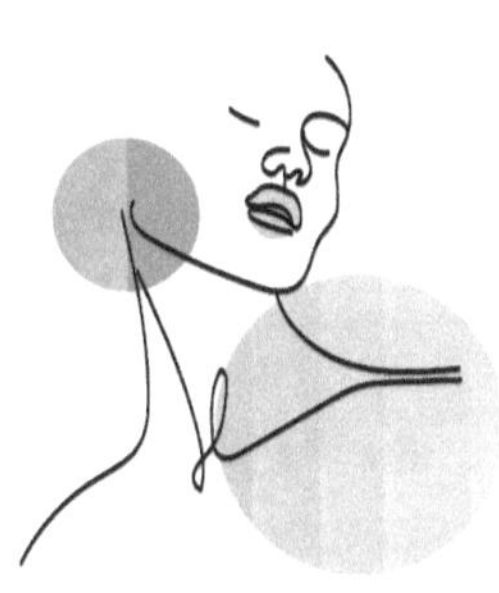

After the wall of the downpour
-the oppressive stillness:
nerves numb with tectonic overload.
All's fine - and yet isn't.
Nightmares have jigged past,
paranoia settled in straight jacket
of stark reality.
Arrows miss the bullseye-
if there be any arrows right now,
and -the bull's eye??

Well here I am
all washed and ironed and
full baked
-but with sour mouth
and bitter mind.
I'm sad I'm glad, and glad I'm sad
and walk the tightrope
strung on hooked question marks...
...what do I feel, someone tell me ...

So this is the respite,
quiet interval between
high tide, low tide.
Here's the equilibrium, the oblique
reality I have to live.

27. Deft Definitions

I

Paranoia...

The demented horse, mane flying,

Nostrils smoking,

Breaks loose and charges

At imagined devils.

II

Sensitivity *has antennae*

That quiver,
That quiver right through
All reason, all sanity.

III

Unhappiness *needs no name,*
It is already known, as pain,
Regret, rejection,
Humiliation,
Defeat.

28. Chitty is Dead

What can one say of death?
It is the only finality we know of
in this world of restlessness and change.
We know it comes sometime, somehow,
Can feel it creep into bones, marrow, brain,
And spread webs on heart and eyes,
No déjà vu, this, it happens only once,
you never live twice.
In a flash it flashes us down the drain;
With all our wasted years, our wasted tears,
Damaging all the tangents

We had with this world,
We go into another,
there to find some mystery,
of another kind,
clutching us by the neck,
our floundering ship to wreck.
The vapour rises from soul,
fills the void in another world:
Black holes of another nothingness,
another bleak reminder that
nothing, nothing can be final.

29. The Eight

*Life goes on
in the rounds of the infinite eight,
again and again, and again.....
Can't get out of this maze,
this never-ending maze...
I want to let go,
oh, I want it to be so!
But the eight keeps coming back,
albeit with some slack,
to find its twin.
It won't let me go,
and slings me back
into the ever-rotating
tunnel of revolving
words, days, memories,*

omissions, commissions.
We are one.

• 56 •

30. Prayer to Shiva

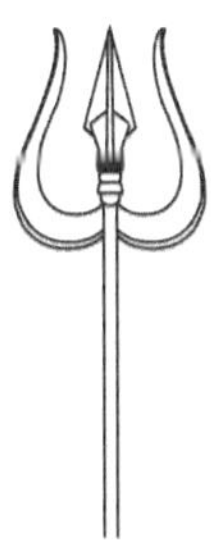

Where have I come, after all these years —
Just full circle? A very narrow circle, indeed!
I just can't get out, I'm shouting for help,
So listen to me oh Shiva! —
to whom I assiduously pray each morning,
burn incense for, put tilak on,
Is it all for nothing,
Or I'm not a good enough disciple,
my veneration lacking blood?
If not,
give me some peace, some mental peace,
In return.
Let me not burn in my private hell,
Please help me out,
help me get out

from the etches and stretches
Of ultimatums in my morbid palm.
Give me a psalm to sing, or a knell to ring,
But get me out of here!

31. Camille Claudel

Such an intense life –
When her love turns to hatred
and turns her mad.
It shows in the torments
of the clay that went
through those fingers
which went through the hair
of a man she thought
would love her,
the way she loved him.
He was, after all, a beast—
butchering up her youth,

he threw her
in the madhouse,
turned her genius to dirt.
She became his fossil, just another creation
Of his lurid lusts.

(Camille Claudel was Rodin's lover and a sculptress of considerable
genius. Rodin's unfaithfulness and rejection finally drove her insane.)

32. The Restless

Restlessness that roams the blood,
leaves vagabond taste on tongue,
makes me leer at conformity,
sneer at narrow living,
I must move, keep moving,
I fear to strike root,
and become a cabbage, carrot, beetroot.
I have to go out, reach out,
feel the length, breadth, volume
of this universe –
Don't want to live life in the

goldfish bowl, on the mantelpiece;
We get away pretty cheap
when we build aquariums
and forget about the sea.
Restless, always on the move,
Can't sit still, always in the groove
No peace, no stability,
No soothing drinks of tranquillity.
Have to strive, have to shine,
have to exhaust body's amphetamine.
That done —
again relapse into silence,
in the pebbles of the sidewalk,
disappear in the shadows
of strange alleys,
there to become just another martyr
to the cause of the dispossessed
— the restless, who own no peace.

33. Phoenix

Monsters that suddenly change sides,
rumble in the caverns of the stomach,
gore her with their bleeding horns:
Wake up to see the truth,
the grimace
that has come upon the mirror,
your reflection merely
the face
of just any other person
in this place.

Every day she strove and strove,

and drove herself down the hill,
for the kill.
But in the depths of the valley,
there it stood, her only goal:
Herself.
She laughed, tried to shrug off the obvious;
Of course, after all, she wanted
only to be herself.

Finally she could the rise from the ashes
and leave behind rebukes, reprimands
lurking in clenched fists, clenched teeth,
and find the freedom not to dwell upon
failures that creased the eyes
and tied her to a past
she could throw away at last.

34. Stranger

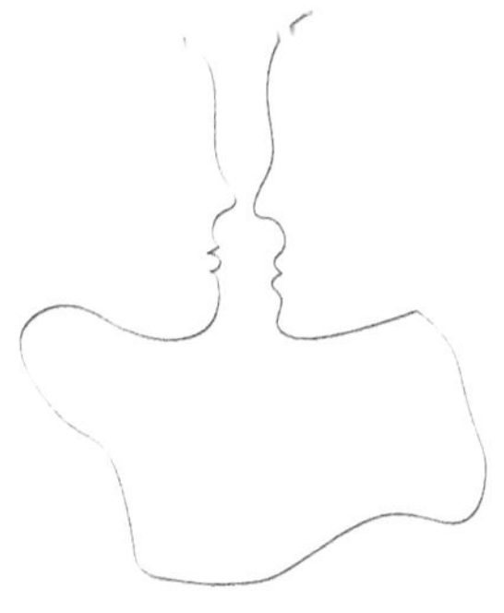

I keep my eyes on the ground,
I fear so much to reveal
the stranger in my eyes,
for it threatens to break
my cornea, my meninges,
and burst over the cliff of my head
and proclaim, proclaim to the world
that it has possessed me.
I try not to speak, this voice is not mine,
It has been silenced by this mute one
that tries hard with monosyllables,
that stumbles on normal talk, normal words,

goes round and round, never-ending,
ever bending the contours of my mind into this black
tunnel of silence.
I fear my violence
may oneday erupt in silence.

35. Loser

From the grey pages,
from the idiot box,
on hoardings outsizing life,
they proclaim it all:
nothing to declare
but our self-confidence.
Bursting at seams, going full steam,
stampeding out the slow,
they are the stars of the show.
You can't be a chooser,
There are no choices to make:
You've got to get to the top,

get a chunk of that cake.
too bad if you flop,
that's your own mistake.

When my son asks me,
Mom, which way should I go?
I'll stare him in the face
and say: how should I know?
I really can't say, son,
I really can't – for,
Son, you are talking to a loser.

36. Daydreamer

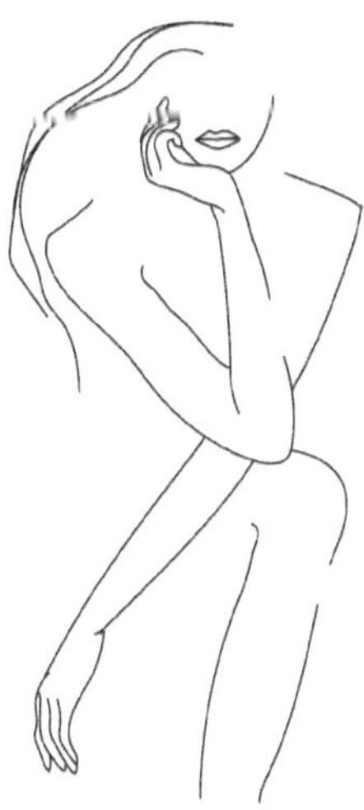

Sometimes the mind races ahead,
displaces time, jumps across boundaries;
I think I am in tomorrow,
when suddenly, I realise
that it's not tomorrow, it's today.
On other days
the shadows of dark secrets
loom large, call me back
into the dense yesterdays.
I regress into the dark undergrowth of many years.

I cannot cope with the onslaught of time,
so I change gears,
slow down, or rev up,
But I am never, never there
to bargain with my todays.

37. Poet's Block

This quiet hour
Is what I wait for
What I work for
And when it comes
I let it slip by
Pen in hand,
Contemplating the gradual
Clotting of ink,
Like disowned blood
In my veins.

38. Working Woman

How can I not appreciate
this woman
who leaves behind
her household
to attend to the various
needs of mine?
For me she should be sublime,
— but all I ever tell her
is that she doesn't do enough,
she must do
that bit just more,

she should survive
on that bit just less,
eat leftovers,
wear hand-me-downs,
and be grateful for my largesse.
Without batting an eyelid
I proclaim my
benevolence
with ill conceived
malevolence.

39. Ayodhya...and After

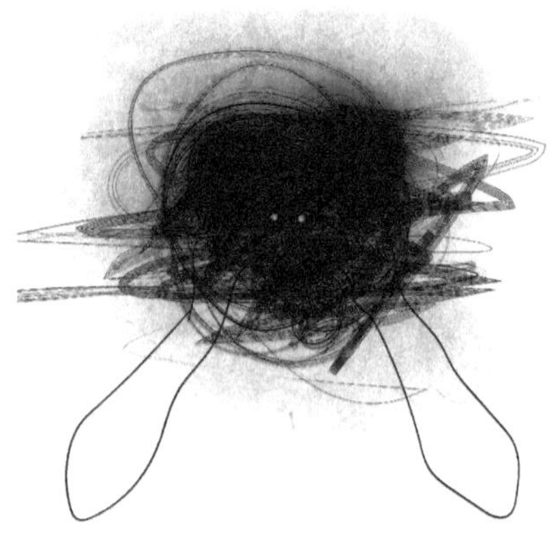

The insane virus breaks lose
and attacks with the ferocity of the mad,
born of demented mind
it has a violence of its own kind.
The madness spreads:
each tooth for tooth, eye for eye, nail for nail,
frothing at mouth corners,
driving itself deathly pale.
It has no religion, it has no shame,
it works incognito,
a crowd has no name.

In the aftermath, we look for solutions,
try to reason things out,
sprinkle magazine pages liberally
with secular logic, semantic balm.
But next time the madness begins,
no ones going to give a damn!

40. North Block

I never fail to get lost here:
so many gates, so many corridors,
so many room numbers,
so many stiff collars.
The other day I went round and round,
right and left and left and right,
and when I finally found his room,
the officer concerned had taken flight!
I cursed my fate and his fate too,
I cursed North Block, what else could I do?
Well, I commenced my tedious journey back,
clickety-click, left, right, left,
and when I finally found the gate,
I had sprouted horns, my hooves were cleft!
I guess North Block is made for the babu's games
of hide and seek and pass the ball,
it's a virtual bureaucratic maze,
it's the toughest one of them all!

(North Block is a building in New Delhi, India housing the offices of the
top bureaucrats in the country.)

41. Ad Infinitum...

The day turns around on itself
devouring the last hours quickly,
impatient for an ending...
that begins yet another cycle.
If only eternity was not so predictable...

Moments run into another,
breath upon breath,
thoughts woven into each other.
I run away from tense

only to find the present
falling behind
into oblivion,
and the future
waiting for the next movement.

42. Quid Pro Quo

Rage, you have such a hold over me,
you spring suddenly on my unsuspecting back
and completely overwhelm me.
My gentle self disappears
and now emerges in your colours:
black, singed at the corners,
fuming from mouth and nose.
Vicious tongue now beheads
the timid flowers of reason,
As a crescendo of lunacy
racks and ravages all sanity,
and makes impulse my sword

my tongue, a battering ram...

But all this I shall inherit in kind,
for,
karma will follow me around doggedly,
sniffing at each and every thought,
word, action,
to give back in good measure
that which I refuse to claim just now,
but must accept gratis, soon enough.

43. Gone

When they said you were about to leave,
I didn't realize it would be so sudden-
-you left without the usual byes-
you slipped away...
and left us gasping in shock.

When I saw you next day
you were the ice maiden-
all laid out like snow white -
peaceful, eerie, not quite you.

I wondered where the light had gone
and how happy would be that land?

Before I knew it,that pack of
village women were upon you
pulling you apart, your lifeless
body defenceless, uncomplaining.
Pushed into the melee, I quietly
played the role of the painter
of nails
and lips,
slipping in the tulsi with water and a
piece of your gold ring for your life hereafter.

One eye glinted and looked
somewhere no one had ever been.
The pain of the years fell away
as you were stripped and bandaged
in new pink clothes.
The blouse with only the neckline
pulled down over your head
as if you had always worn it
unstitched...
your saree draped shoddily
over your compliant limbs
that still tried some protest
in rigor mortis.

And so they took you away
with band ,baaja, and pomp you
never saw in your lifetime,
with hundreds
of multicoloured shawls piled high
on your cold form
to keep you warm.

I watched the departure and
lost no time in ravaging
your belongings,
commenting wryly at the modest finds.

44. Letting Go

I should have known by now
how you dislike these
bouts of mania.
Your life is lived
in the slots of predictability,
creases all ironed out,
ruffled feathers plucked and discarded.
I should have learnt by now
that you don't like these displays
of vulnerability,
that set you on edge

and cramp your alphaness.
You'd rather move on
without the drag
of heavy custody.
So I let you free...
I shall never let
the knots of my needs
tie you down again.

The Poet

Renu Singh Parmar

Renu Singh Parmar is a retired officer of the Indian Economic Service and has been writing poetry ever since she can remember. She is also a painter and storyteller.

Her first collection of poems, **Ovarian Sentiments** was published by Writer's Workshop in 1993 and the second, **Off The Radar** by BUUKS in 2020.

Her poems have also been published in the anthology *Poetry India-Voices in the Making* by Arnold Publishers.

She is also the author of **All For Something**, a collection of short stories, and **Whispers to Yogananda** her devotional poem offerings to her Guru, both published by Notionpress in 2021.